Naughty Hap

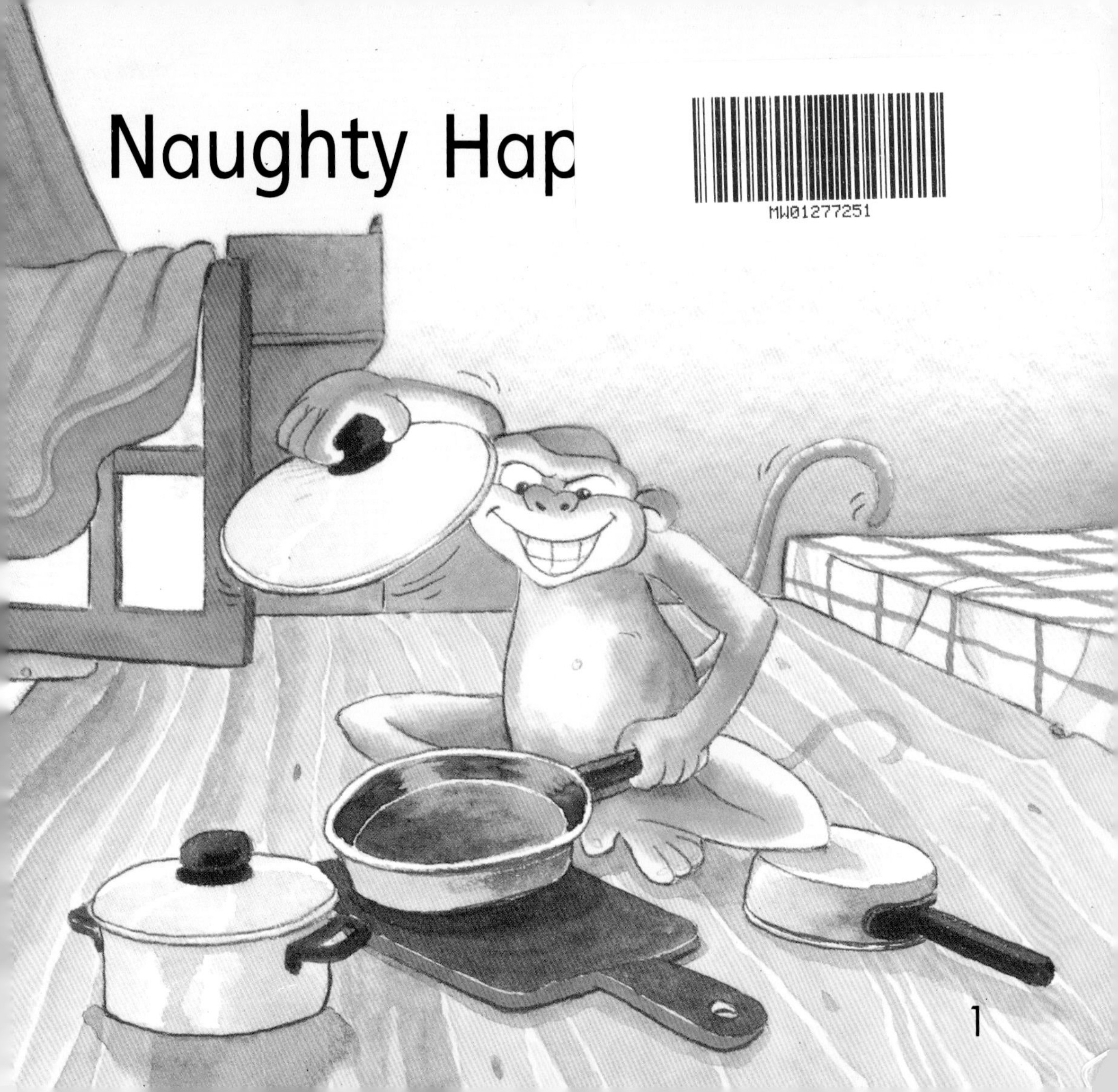

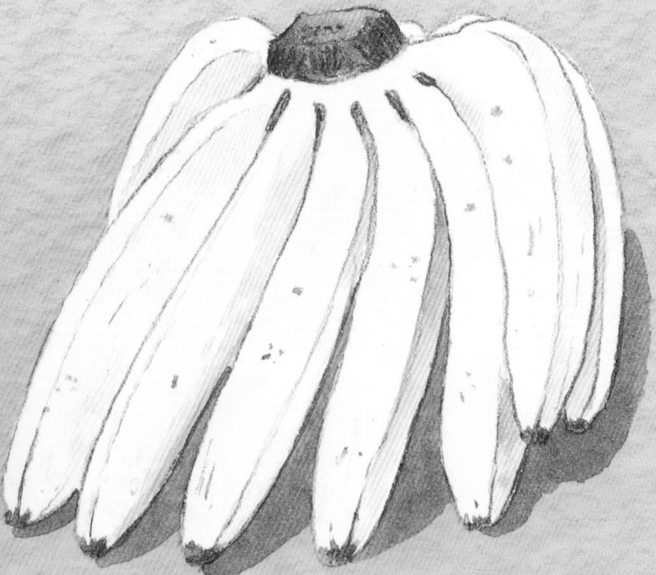

Where are the bananas?

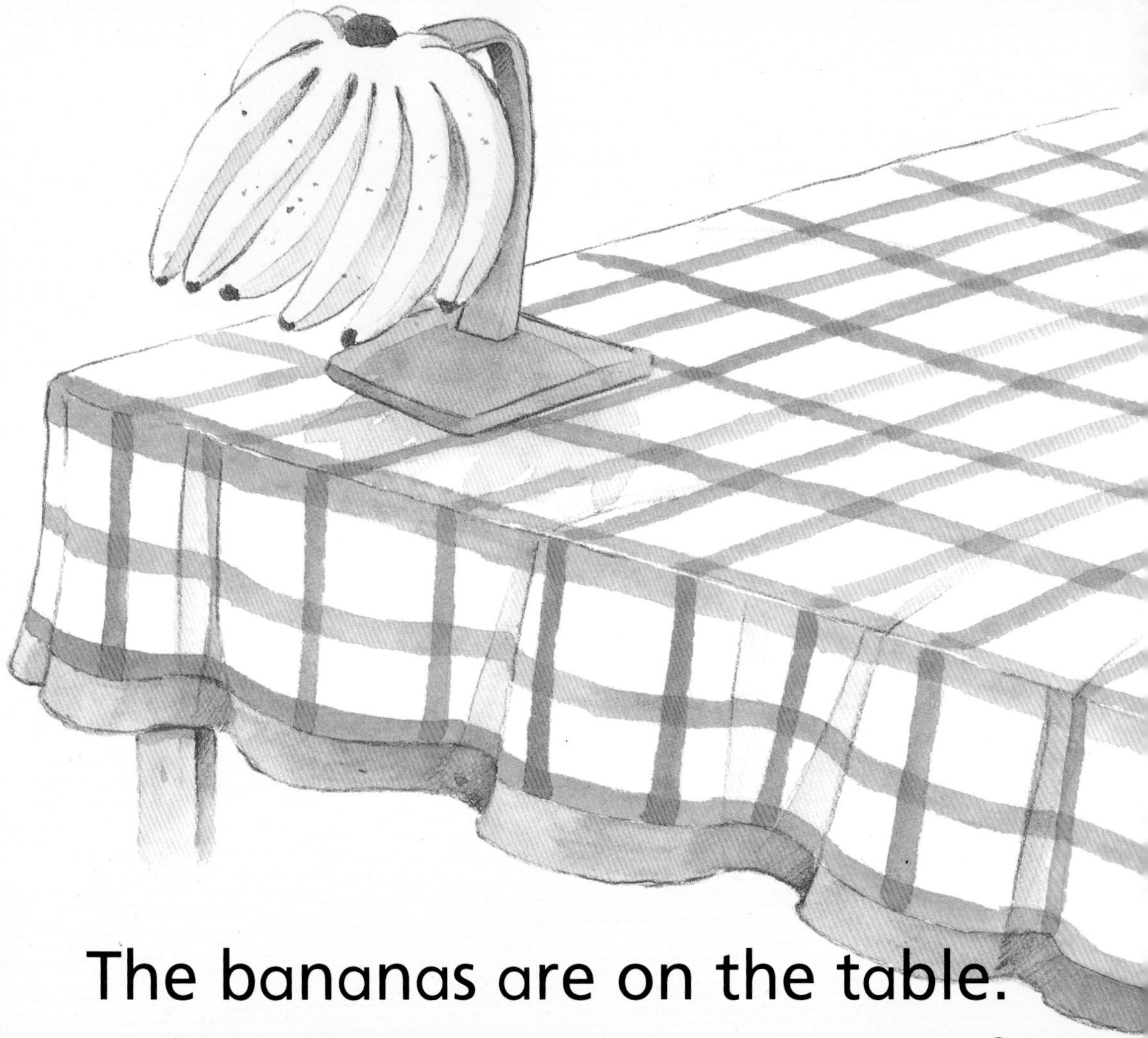

The bananas are on the table.

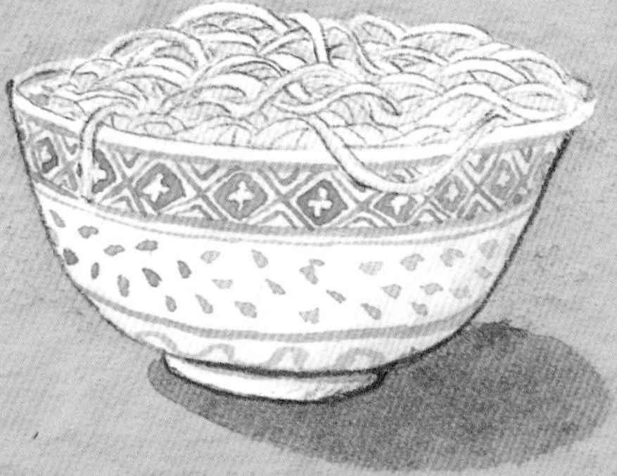

Where are the noodles?

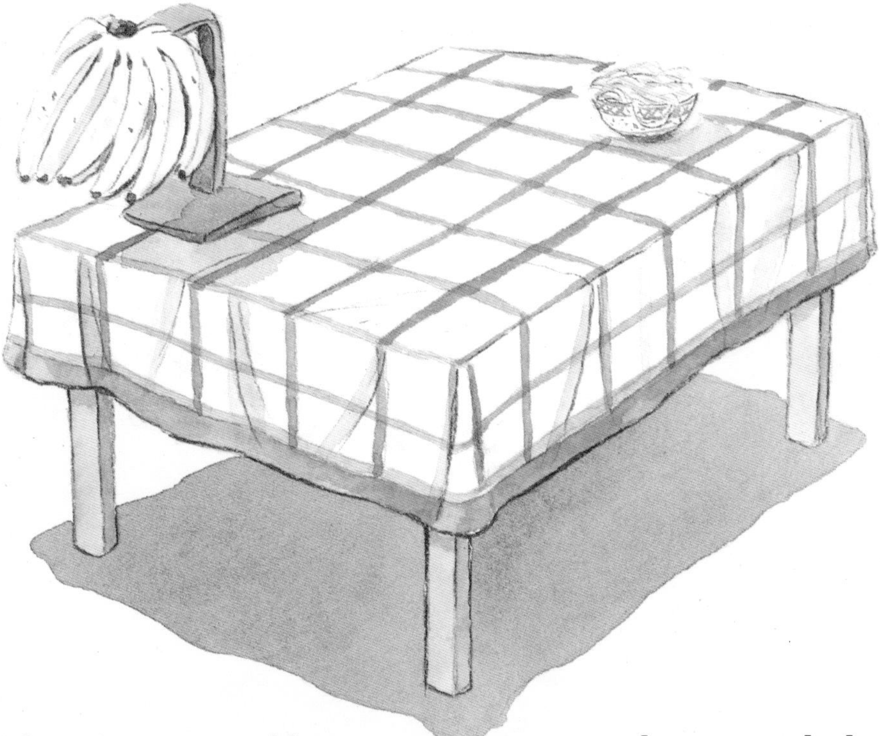

The noodles are on the table.

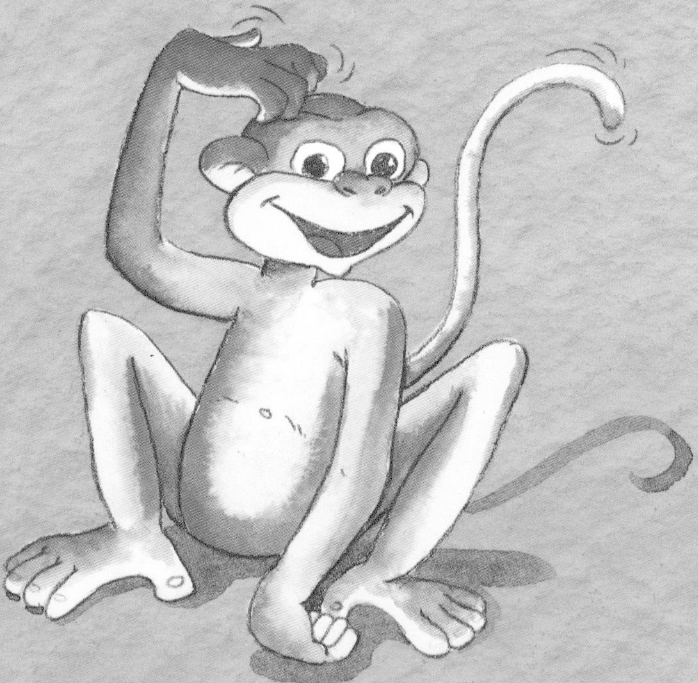

Where is Happy Monkey?

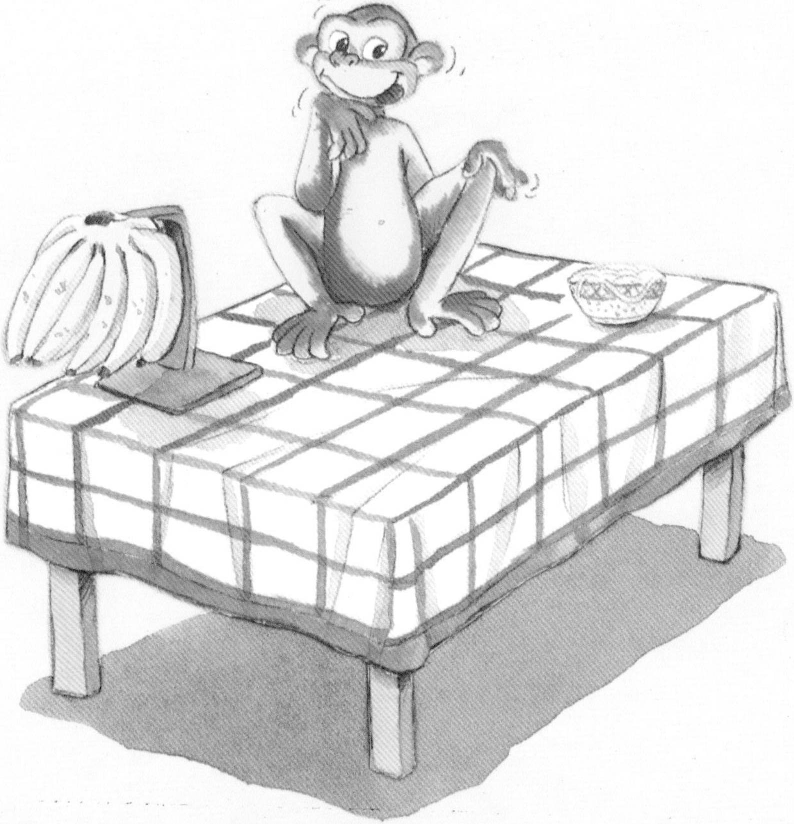

Happy Monkey is on the table.

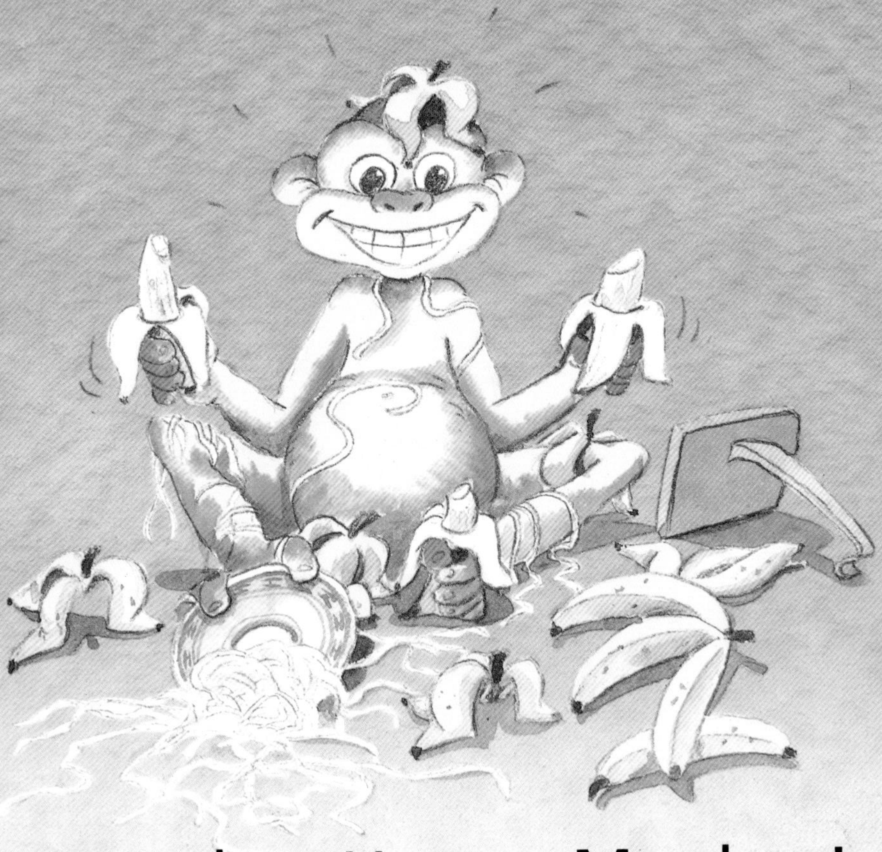

Naughty Happy Monkey!